HF270662

# CANCER

by Elizabeth Andrews

This book is filled with videos, puzzles, games, and more! Scan the QR codes* while you read, or visit the website below to make this book pop.

popbooksonline.com/cancer


abdobooks.com

Published by Pop!, a division of ABDO, PO Box 398166, Minneapolis, Minnesota 55439. Copyright © 2026 by Abdo Consulting Group, Inc. International copyrights reserved in all countries. No part of this book may be reproduced in any form without written permission from the publisher. DiscoverRoo™ is a trademark and logo of Pop!.

Printed in the United States of America, North Mankato, Minnesota.

042025
082025

Cover Photo: Splendoura Prints; Shutterstock Images
Interior Photos: Getty Images; Shutterstock Images
Editor: Tyler Gieseke
Series Designer: Laura Graphenteen

**Library of Congress Control Number: 2024948395**

**Publisher's Cataloging-in-Publication Data**
Names: Andrews, Elizabeth, author.
Title: Cancer / by Elizabeth Andrews
Description: Minneapolis, Minnesota : Pop!, 2026 | Series: Zodiac signs | Includes online resources and index
Identifiers: ISBN 9781098247881 (lib. bdg.) | ISBN 9781098248420 (ebook)
Subjects: LCSH: Cancer (Astrology)--Juvenile literature. | Crab (Astrology)--Juvenile literature. | Zodiac--Juvenile literature. | Astrology--Juvenile literature. | Astrology--Charts, diagrams, etc.--Juvenile literature.
Classification: DDC 133.52--dc23


*Scanning QR codes requires a web-enabled smart device with a QR code reader app and a camera.

# TABLE OF CONTENTS

# MEET THE CANCER!

Cancer is the fourth sign of the zodiac.

People born between June 22 and July 22 are Cancerians. When people ask for your "star sign," they are likely asking for your sun sign. This is the zodiac sign the sun appeared in at your birth.

*White Rose*

# CANCER

constellation

3

numbers

7

# ZODIAC CALENDAR

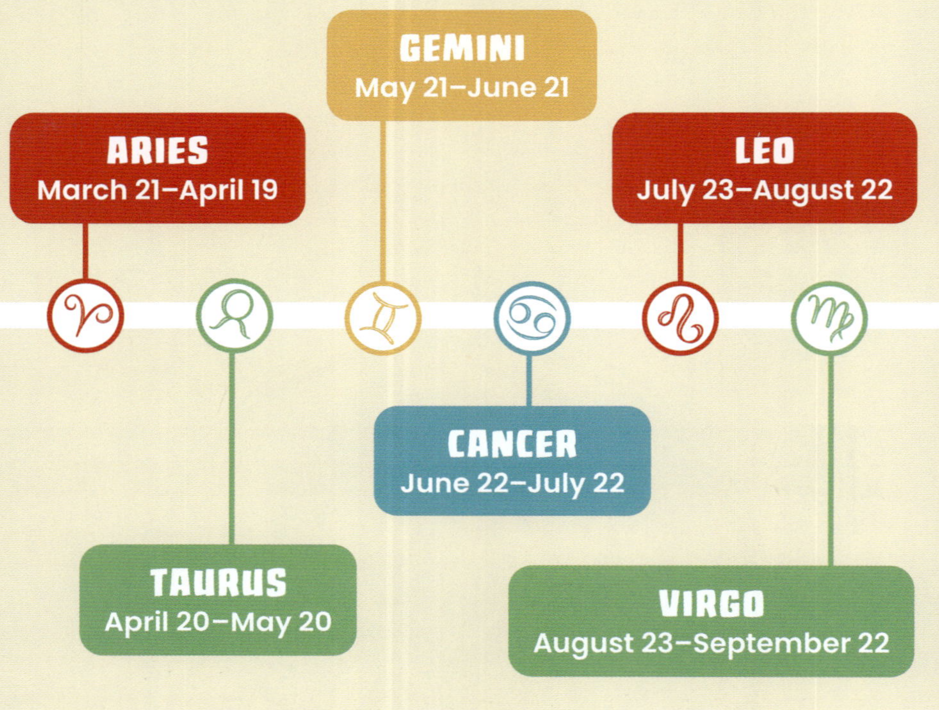


Three features help describe zodiac signs. Signs can be masculine or feminine. Each zodiac sign is given a mode. The three modes are cardinal, fixed, and mutable. Each zodiac is also

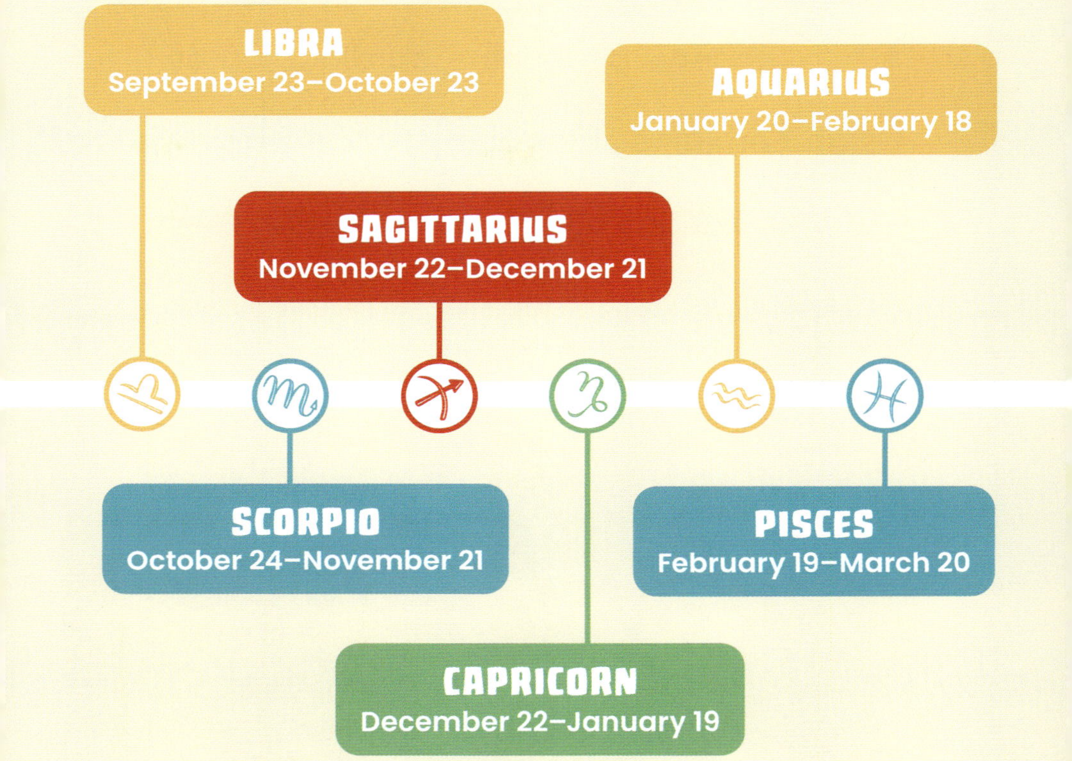


a fire, air, earth, or water sign. No zodiac sign shares the same three features.

**DID YOU KNOW?**

Cardinal signs are leaders in friend groups.

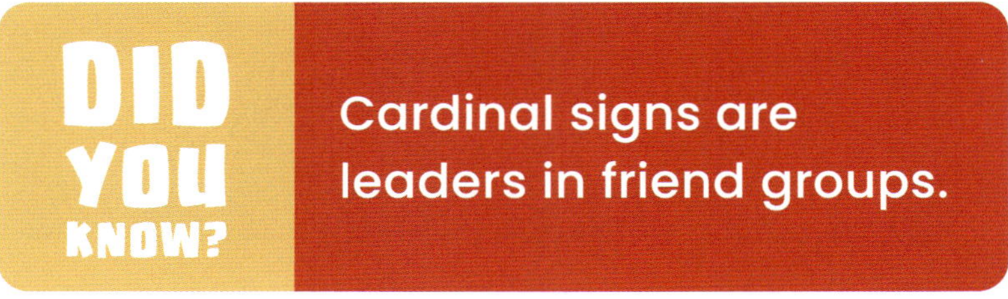

Cancer is a feminine, cardinal, water sign. Feminine signs are grounded. Many of their actions are done **internally**. They are in touch with their own emotions and those around them.

*Feminine signs might need more time alone.*

*Cardinal signs are born at the beginning of seasons.*

Modes describe how signs interact with the outside world. Having a cardinal sign means a Cancerian enjoys trying new things. A Cancerian is quick to act when an idea strikes. Water signs are emotional and observant. They are often **sentimental** and **sensitive**.

The monster Hercules fought was called a hydra. It had many heads.

Cancer is **represented** by the crab. The ancient Greeks believed Cancer's **constellation** was the giant crab who pinched the hero Hercules. Hercules was fighting a monster in a swamp. The goddess Hera wanted Hercules to lose, so she ordered the crab to hurt Hercules. The crab was crushed during the fight. Hera placed the crab among the stars in thanks.

*Crabs belong to a group of animals called crustaceans.*

# HISTORY OF ASTROLOGY

Humans have looked for life's **spiritual** meaning since the beginning of time. They often looked to the stars for this. Astrology is the practice of reading the movements of planets and other **celestial** bodies and connecting them to life on Earth.

*Some ancient people used the zodiac signs to predict future events.*

Babylonians invented the zodiac in Mesopotamia over 5,000 years ago. Mesopotamia was the first known civilization. Babylon was one of the region's largest cities.

14

The zodiac is a belt of space around Earth that has 12 well-known **constellations**. Ancient people noticed that the sun seemed to move in front of these constellations throughout a year. The sun spends about a month in each constellation.

The constellations in the zodiac belt are Aries, Taurus, Gemini, Cancer, Leo, Virgo, Libra, Scorpius, Sagittarius, Capricornus, Aquarius, and Pisces. Together they make up the 12 zodiac signs. They are all **represented** by different **symbols**.

*Islamic astrologers created new ways to map and measure stars.*

# THE ZODIAC WHEEL

Most zodiac symbols are animals. The ancient Greeks called the belt of space *zodiakos kyklos*, or "circle of animals."

# CHAPTER 3

# RULED BY FEELINGS

Cancer is the only sign ruled by the moon.

The moon **represents** the thoughts and feelings deep in a person's mind. The moon is a very feminine **celestial** body.

It is sometimes called "Mother Moon."

Cancerians are faithful and loving people. They like to care for those they love.

Cancerians have a
hard time when they
are separated from
loved ones.

Like the ocean's tides are controlled by the moon, Cancerians are controlled by their emotions. They often try to keep their emotions hidden. But their feelings are powerful and easily take over. Sometimes this makes Cancerians feel out of control. They often believe they are making things up as they go while everyone else knows exactly what they are doing.

*All water signs have qualities that resemble certain types of water. Cancerians are like ocean waves.*

*Cancerians get their feelings hurt easily.*

Cancerians are **sentimental** people. A song on the radio or a certain smell brings them back in time. Sometimes, Cancerians are called the "cosmic collectors." This means they keep memories, friends, and things that are special to them forever.

*Cancerians enjoy hearing other people's stories.*

Cancerians crave security. As the cosmic collectors, they keep things close to them that make them happy. They like to feel familiar with their surroundings. Cancerians' favorite place to be is at home with the people they love.

While Cancerians get lost in positive emotions, they can also get lost in negative ones. They get grumpy easily. If something is bothering them, or if a task is more difficult than they expected, Cancerians are often moody.

*Michael Phelps is a Cancerian. He has the most Olympic medals ever. He is known for opening up about his emotions.*

# A CANCERIAN'S JUDGMENT

Cancerians are very observant. This means they pay close attention to what happens around them. Cancerians react emotionally to their observations. They make quick judgments on new

*Pearls represent love and the search for wisdom.*

people and places. Often, Cancerians'

judgments are correct. Because of this,

people trust Cancerians.

Like their **symbol**, the crab, Cancerians have hard outer shells. They use their shells for protection. They need protection because they are soft and **sentimental** on the inside.

Cancerians are kind. They are good listeners and easily understand how others are feeling. These are skills they get from being ruled by the moon. When people need them, they are willing to help. They like to fix people's problems and make sure everyone around them is happy. Friends of Cancerians might describe them as mother hens.

*Cancer is the hardest zodiac constellation to see.*

Malala Yousafzai is a Cancerian. She has worked to help girls around the world get an education.

As a doctor, Cancerians could use their power of observation to help people.

Cancerians' kindness and **sensitivity** make them a good fit for caring and healing jobs. They could be doctors or counselors. Cancerians are also creative and have big imaginations. They would do well in careers in the arts.

Today, astrology can answer questions about an individual. People use astrology to understand who they are and why they might do what they do. It can also help them understand other people in their life. A zodiac sign can point out personal skills, possibilities, and **internal motivations**.

### TEXT-TO-SELF

Are you a Cancerian? If so, do you think the sign matches your personality? If not, what do you have in common with Cancerians?

### TEXT-TO-TEXT

Have you read any books about the other zodiac signs? How were those signs similar to and different from Cancer?

### TEXT-TO-WORLD

With the help of an adult, look up famous Cancerians. Pick one person and write a few sentences about ways that person shows Cancerian qualities.

# GLOSSARY

**celestial** — having to do with the sky or outer space.

**constellation** — a group of stars that forms a pattern.

**internal** — of, relating to, or being on the inside.

**motivation** — something that makes one want to do something.

**psychic** — having special mental abilities such as seeing the future or knowing others' thoughts.

**represent** — to stand for or be a sign of.

**sensitive** — feeling or noticing things quite sharply.

**sentimental** — causing or showing tender feelings.

**spiritual** — having to do with people's beliefs in things such as the soul, nature, and what happens after death.

**symbol** — an object or picture that represents something else.

# INDEX

This book is filled with videos, puzzles, games, and more! Scan the QR codes* while you read, or visit the website below to make this book pop.

popbooksonline.com/cancer

*Scanning QR codes requires a web-enabled smart device with a QR code reader app and a camera.